THE RECIPE OF A STRONG WOMAN

By

LATERRA Nicole HOWARD

Copyright © 2021 by LaTerra Howard

ISBN: 978-0-578-88499-8

All rights reserved. This book or any portion thereof may not be reproduced or used in any manner whatsoever without the express written permission of the publisher except for the use of brief quotations in a book review.

DEDICATION

Taji and Amaya, my heart and soul. You two inspire me more than you could ever imagine. You both have been my motivation for everything I have done and continue to do. I hope I have made you proud. I love you with everything I have inside of me, Thank you.

In Loving Memory of Alice Lowe

For helping me make this book possible I thank,

God for giving me the strength I needed when times were rough.

MHB, for giving me the courage to color outside of the lines. I will forever be grateful. I love you deep, you will always have my heart.

Jean P. Gibson, my mother, for always allowing me to be myself. I love you.

Charles Gibson, my father, I appreciate all that you have done and continue to do. I love you.

Michael and Torrone, my brothers, for always believing in me. I love you both to the very end.

Jaleah, my little superwoman, for showing up and saving the day. I Love you much.

My family and friends, thanks for routing me on and praying for me when needed. You are all greatly appreciated.

To all the strong women, this was written for you with much love and gratitude. Continue to soar high.

PRESENTED TO:

_____

FROM:

_____

DATE:

_____

CONTENTS

THE MAKINGS OF A STRONG WOMAN 1

NAVIGATING RELATIONSHIPS 12

UNDERSTANDING SUCCESS AND FAILURES . . . 25

ACCEPTING RESPONSIBILITY 38

PERSONAL GROWTH 48

SELF-LOVE 60

NEW BEGINNINGS 71

THE MAKINGS OF

A STRONG WOMAN

A strong woman is loving, compassionate, enduring, and courageous. You can do anything that you set your mind to.

A strong woman must understand that someone else's blessings were designed especially for them. You should not want what they were provided. You must recognize that everything is not meant for everyone. Concentrate on your own garden; your budding may just be blossoming a tad bit slower creating your own unique flowers.

A strong woman always has a story that needs to be shared. Some words written are positive, while others appear negative. Either way, the opinions of others should never deter you from your authentic character. Do not live worrying about how others portray you, just continue staying true to your script. Remember your screenplay was designed especially for you, and only you have the rights to your biography.

A strong woman knows doing what you said you were going to do is simply a sign of integrity. There should never be an excuse for staying true to your word. That is a gratification that shall come from within, this helps with building character. Without character or honest words, there will never be anything for others to rely on, or nothing for you to stand on. Your word is everything, that is how you shape the platform to becoming a trustworthy, reliable woman.

A strong woman understands that she must lead by example. In order to be a great leader, you must guide by what you do, not only by what you say. Remember perception comes from expectation, and before expecting, it must first be shown to the projected.

A strong woman must expect the unexpected, acknowledging there are going to be times when things do not seem to go as planned. When that occurs, it is necessary for you to give yourself time to make the proper adjustments. Once made, begin planning your future possibilities

A strong woman must identify with the unbalanced areas within your life. Begin by dissecting the issues you are faced with, familiarize yourself with your burdens, then determine what needs to be done to fix the problem. It does not matter whether it is your employment, your family, a friendship, or a relationship. This situation may require some detachment, even if it is momentarily. You must determine whether the solution to your decision should be kept temporarily or made permanently. No matter what your choices are, only you need to be satisfied by the outcome. Even if that means you must lose someone or something.

A strong woman often lives life as an open book. Some chapters may come off a bit humorous, while others seem more mysterious. Certain chapters become thrilling, while others turn into sultry romances. So, enjoy reading every single page knowing a greater chapter lies ahead. Remember, no matter how the chapter plays out, each one must end and soon enough the story will be over.

A strong woman must understand sometimes you must follow to receive the knowledge to lead. It is ok to take the backseat while learning a new route. Following the right leader will help guide you to the right destination and give you the confidence and courage needed to acquire the driver's seat.

A strong woman may take time for granted; always thinking you have more. Take the initiative to pursue your dreams and stop procrastinating with your future. To achieve success, you need to be equipped with determination and have discipline to see it through.

NAVIGATING RELATIONSHIPS

A strong woman needs to understand jealousy can creep into any great relationship, revealing itself in the most untraditional ways. You must acknowledge someone else's misfortune does not have anything to do with you. Keep being exactly who you are, continue working hard, and never slow down. Do not allow the insecurities of others to make you feel uneasy about celebrating you, your achievements, or your success.

A strong woman must learn to let go of negativity. Cleanse your thoughts, while clearing up your mind. If you are unsatisfied with anything or anyone that is bringing you down, now is the time to release yourself from those situations. Once you are free, the authentic you will resurface. Now that is something you will have to look forward too.

A strong woman must understand that dealing with miserable people most often becomes contagious. You must remember that when interacting with them, it can easily contaminate your spirit. Only you have the power to delegate what is acceptable to enter your mental capacity and being miserable should not be accepted or allowed.

A strong woman knows that when a relationship ends it can become extremely difficult. The decision-making process itself can be the crucial part. Obtaining the confidence to leave, becomes even more challenging. Once you can overcome the distress of that obstacle, you can begin to understand your decision. The releasing part will allow you to loosen that anchor that was once holding you down. Now comes the time to heal, take whatever time you need.

A strong woman needs to understand that nothing or no one enters your life accidentally. Remember that behind each interaction, there is an experience. All experiences turn into lessons. With each lesson, you are taught something that you can carry on with you throughout your life. Try your best to sustain it all because once it is over, all you have left is the memories.

A strong woman understands that there will be a time when someone tries to take away the sparkle from your happiness. Everyone around you should be as happy as you are when your moment arrives the same way you are happy for theirs. Understand that whoever it is that tries to steal your joy for the wrong reasons must no longer be a part of the plan.

A strong woman should never settle just for the sake of saying you are in a relationship. Do not stick around just to feel like you are a part of something. Relationships come with real obligations, everyone involved should have certain expectations. From the very beginning each person should know what is wanted and expected to sustain the courtship. That decision must be conveyed from the very start so everyone's request can be met. If by chance your partner is no longer interested in keeping up with their end of the bargain, do not just walk away, take time to review what their new desires are. If their sudden change in behavior is nonnegotiable, then the only decision left is for the contract to be null and voided. Keep in mind there will always be another prospect willing to meet your standards, no matter how high your expectations are set.

A strong woman must know when to stop making yourself available for people that are unavailable to you. Understand, effort works in both directions. When you start to feel like you are giving too much of yourself in the relationship, and you are not feeling appreciated, begin pulling yourself back. Start by changing your perspective, it is ok to spend more time on yourself. You may even discover how much you adore it. Just remember, people will forever find the time for anything of importance to them. Unfortunately, if you are not a part of their time, you did not make their cut. Respect their decision and be fine with the fact you may have to move along, even if it means being alone.

A strong woman must understand how you feel is not the only way to sustain a healthy relationship. You must also be aware of what your needs are. Ask yourself, are you really receiving what you deserve? Just because people may enter your life in what seems like the right way does not mean they cannot have the wrong intentions. Although the feelings you have may appear to be love, remember to study their actions. Actions always speak volumes. Love should never hurt nor should it disrespect. Be strong while understanding feelings can fade, but respect will last you a lifetime.

A strong woman must realize there is a purpose for everyone that enters your life. Some will appear to show you what you have been missing all along. While others may appear just to challenge you. Then there are the ones whose sole purpose for coming around is to try and use you. They come around from the very beginning looking for a handout, never wanting to be a part of the contribution. Those are the ones that are there for you to realize what is not needed.

No matter what your encounters were, always look at it as a learning experience. In the end, only you can decide whether their intentions are good or bad for you, and who is granted permanent access to stay or go.

A strong woman should never walk away regretting how much you have given in any relationship. Especially, when you know your intentions were genuine, and your heart was pure. If you did what was right during the process, it is not up to you to worry about the other individual. Accept whatever consequences come with any decision you need to make. Understand people are not always going to treat you the way they should. Acknowledge their imperfections, forgive their uncertainties, and just move on.

A strong woman must understand when choosing your mate, it should be someone that will empower you, wholeheartedly love you, solely support you, and genuinely inspire you. Even if the person you are currently with cannot love you in that capacity, it does not mean they are not a good person. Maybe you two are just not compatible. No matter what do not lose faith, the person you deserve will eventually appear. Until then, just continue working effortlessly on yourself so you can be prepared when that special moment arrives.

UNDERSTANDING SUCCESS AND FAILURES

A strong woman often deals with struggles and disappointment. No matter what happens, you cannot give up. Remember, everyone is dealt a different set of cards. Strategically, you must continue playing the hand you were dealt. Stay strong during each shuffle, while keeping your confidence. Have faith knowing the game only ends when you stop playing.

A strong woman that works hard and diligently, knows efforts may go unnoticed. Never let that deter you from doing your absolute best. Not being acknowledged may become discouraging at times but keep moving forward. Keep in mind, all your efforts may not earn certain honors. Even if it is overlooked, learn to be okay with that and never doubt yourself.

A strong woman must learn to replace negative thoughts with positive thoughts to allow better results throughout your life. Thinking more positively in your decision making will become more rewarding with less annoyance. Focus on all the good things you have going on instead of dwelling on the negative. Even your so-called failures can be turned into self-rewarding lessons.

A strong woman must be aware that when one door of happiness closes, another one eventually opens. Often your concentration is focused on negativity, you are too worried about the shut door. Which is making it exceedingly difficult for you to see another door that has been slowly opening right in front of you. Stop worrying about what could have been and proceed living for now.

A strong woman must be persistent as well as aggressive when going after your dreams. You will eventually reach the realization that "No" should never be an option. Each day will welcome a new beginning and your perspective on life will begin to shift with realization that "Yes" is on the way.

A strong woman must never wish for the downfall of others. Hoping for another person's failures only demoralizes you and who you are. Just because things are not going in your favor now, does not give you the right to diminish another person's blessings. Instead try to be understanding and appreciate what you do have. They may appear to have it all, but you may never know what type of struggles they had to endure to get where they are. So be kind, while cheering them on, because you never know what prayers are being prayed for you.

A strong woman often deals with daily trials and tribulations, while balancing the politics of everyday life. Sometimes it is embraced with a smile but most often it is concealed with your tears. No matter what issues you are faced with, always deal with it while holding your head high. Remember, each day will end with a new one to follow. Which means all your problems from today will not be a concern tomorrow.

A strong woman must understand that even if you fail your first time around, you cannot give up. Success often comes after you try and try again. Nothing or no one shall ever force you to give up, including yourself. Never stop until you reach the goal you have been waiting to achieve. No matter how long it takes for you to reach it, once you receive it, you will have a greater respect for your challenging work, knowing it did not come easy. You will then be able to walk away feeling more confident than you ever have.

A strong woman is sometimes afraid of achieving success. Maybe the thought of conquering your accomplishment scares you because you think you do not deserve it. Once you understand that everything you have mastered is because of all your hard work, and that is a celebration. You will soon be able to accept it by coming into your own. That is when you will face the fear that what you have professed is worthy of all your achievements.

A strong woman must take the initiative to understand financial literacy. You must learn the importance of your dollar. This knowledge will equip you with the necessary tools needed for your financial journey. Once this is understood, it will assist you to sustain a solid financial foundation to begin creating generational wealth. Which eventually can be passed on for other's personal gain.

A strong woman knows balance can sometimes become a struggle. You often take on way more than you should, thinking you can handle it. Trying to keep up with all the different areas of your life can be overwhelming. Practice self-discipline so you may continue to be multifaceted without wasting time or procrastinating. Everything will not always be perfect but there will always be areas for self-improvement and growth.

A strong woman can sometimes forget where she came from. You may be ashamed of your past or do not like the road you traveled on to get to your destination. Either way that is your story it is encouraged to be shared. Instead of feeling unworthy, own it, and be strong while standing tall. Tell your story, you may just be the inspiration that someone else needed on their road to recovery.

ACCEPTING RESPONSIBILITY

A strong woman must take full responsibility once a decision has been made, whether right or wrong. No one other than yourself should be held accountable for your mistakes. Understand mistakes are made to be corrected, not to be distributed onto others. Once your errors are acknowledged, it becomes easier for you to accept. Now comes the time for you to make the necessary changes needed for the reversal and correction of your blunders.

A strong woman sometimes risks it all by taking chances. Be brave enough to understand it may not always turn out the way you may expect it. Be strong enough to accept the conclusion once it is over. Be wise enough to develop in areas you were never interested in correcting. Now go ahead and fix those issues you have been waiting patiently to resolve.

A strong woman must find the courage to say "NO" to people and things that are no longer beneficial. This is the time for you to release, reevaluate, and rediscover yourself while accepting the decisions you have made. Then, it is up to you if you decide to keep wasting time.

A strong woman accepts the importance of admitting when she is wrong. It takes a certain type of confidence to accept your flaws, while owning them. Acceptance is not only a sign of growth; it gives you a sense of solidity. In life, it is not always about being right. There comes a time when you must be willing to put aside your pride and acknowledge it is ok to be mistaken, while moving along in your self-development.

A strong woman needs to understand that opportunity may not always come knocking. You need to have the willingness to go out there and the drive to search for it. Seek the different areas in your life that need a change. Allow each experience you meet to become your gateway to discovering something far greater. Once your mind taps into your hidden potential, you will realize you have a gem in your situation.

A strong woman must acknowledge their individual shortcomings by accepting all their flaws. There should never be an issue when it comes to working on yourself. Your goal should never be trying to change someone else, that is their job to carry out. If individuality change is not what the other person is looking to do, be ok with it, because in the end their battle is not yours to fight. Just continue working effortlessly on your own necessary changes. Do not give up no matter how difficult it may become. You will eventually reach the finish line, and once that is carried out, you should be the only one to reap the benefits of your self-improvement.

A strong woman knows being happy does not always mean you are where you would like to be in life. It just means you are accepting where you are, but you are also willing to take the necessary steps needed for you to meet your goals. Once you reach your destination, you will continue the road you have paved for yourself, which will eventually turn into pure bliss.

A strong woman must understand being a toxic person often influences the ones around you. Although your light seems to be dim, you cannot allow the darkness to make you bitter. Instead confront whatever issues you may be having, then hold yourself accountable for your own actions. Even when you feel you are on the urge of bending, never break, or give up, just keep fighting things will get better.

A strong woman needs to realize that sometimes you are the selfish one in the relationship. Instead of always deflecting your wants onto others, try challenging yourself to understand you cannot always be the one on the receiving end. Imagine how the other person may feel. Begin accepting responsibility while trying to get to the root of your problems. While you are on the path of improving as a person, just hope you are not losing influential people.

PERSONAL GROWTH

A strong woman understands forgiving someone who has hurt you is a great way to continue this journey of life. Forgiving does not necessarily show a sign of weakness; it shows a declaration of strength. Acknowledge that forgiveness will never be about the other person; it will always be about you. Once you forgive, the pain in your heart will begin to release. Allowing you more space for the healing of your mind, and the confidence to let go.

A strong woman, who gets to know themselves better, often identifies an area of internal change. Stop looking for the wrongdoing in others, begin focusing on your own shortcomings. No one is responsible for taking care of you. You are the only one in control of your happiness and mental health.

A strong woman should never walk in someone else's shadow. Stand tall, be yourself, while learning who you are. Begin taking the necessary steps needed to love yourself. Enjoy the embracement of your own identity. Just because you admire someone, does not mean they need a duplication.

A strong woman knows that to be a significant figure in someone else's life, you must first be prevailing in your own. You cannot be there for another individual if you are not submerged in your own growth. Before sharing yourself with others, make sure the gifts that you are offering are worth giving.

A strong woman knows your life can be enriched when you have strength around you. At some point, all women deserve an opportunity to be exposed to a woman who can act as your mentor, confidant, and motivator. Someone who is not afraid to tell you when you are wrong, while having the same ability to tell you when you are right. Having that variability within a person, will not only allow you to grow to be the best version of you, but it gives you the ability to learn how to trust.

A strong woman should never be afraid to make the necessary changes in their life that is needed. The beauty of growing is never feeling an obligation to stay in the same place you were once in. As you begin growing mentally, you will start to outgrow certain things. Some of those situations you never thought was possible for you to live without. Let go because comfortability stagnates you into believing where you are is where you belong. Evolving will allow you possibilities you never knew existed.

A strong woman is often knocked down by multiple life challenges. Do not allow those challenges to keep you down. Continue moving forward, while jumping over your hurdles, and staring your problems directly in the eyes. Credit is never accounted for by giving up, but it does stand for something much greater when you make the effort to keep going.

A strong woman must understand the best relationship you can have is the one you sustain with yourself. For you to be capable of loving anyone else you must already know what it takes. Self-love will teach you the importance of your true happiness. Loving yourself first helps you accept just who you are. While coming to terms with every aspect of your life, even with the things you thought could not be changed. Once those terms are met within yourself, you will genuinely begin to appreciate every aspect of your life and can now disperse the love you have inside.

A strong woman often wants to believe in something they know deep down inside is far from realization. Stop trying to rationalize with lies to make yourself comfortable with not facing the truth. Of course, pretending and make believe is far easier to absorb. There is something about that courage, that always taste a bit sweeter while digesting. Realize it is going to take a lot of confidence if you want to accept reality. Many are not willing or ready to disturb, most would rather just continue living in fantasyland, torn and despondent.

A strong woman must understand it is natural to grieve. Grief is a response you endure when dealing with any loss you may experience. It is the emotional suffering you are faced with when someone or something has been taken away from you. You may even experience your physical health being disrupted. Take all the time you need and know you are not alone. The healing process will be difficult but to except your loss, you must learn to cope with it. How you cope with your loss, can only be determined by you. If outside help is needed, seek it. Always keep in mind whatever it is you are dealing with will soon become easier as you bark on your own road to recovery.

A strong woman understands that it is ok to ask for help. Being independent and capable of satisfying all your needs emotionally, intellectually, and financially are always a plus. However, even the most self-sufficient woman can fall short in certain areas throughout life. When it becomes difficult, it is never about how hard you fall, it is about how fast you get up. Set your pride aside. Go ahead, ask for assistance. You will be surprised by all those who are willing to step in to help pull you back up.

SELF-LOVE

A strong woman needs to have the courage to stand alone. Understand that you do not need anyone to make you feel validated. The validation you are looking for should come from loving yourself, wholeheartedly. Once you obtain that confidence, you will realize that self-love is the greatest reward.

A strong woman that values herself understands she is a gift to anyone she meets. It begins by loving the woman that you are and realizing your full worth. Recognize what you bring to someone's life. Once you understand those components, you will begin believing your worth and your contributions will forever be unmatched.

A strong woman must always celebrate the person you once were, the person you are now, and the person you would love to become. Continue searching until you find her. If you do not go after what you want, you will never fully understand what it feels like to have it. Step up, step out and step forward and begin following your dreams so you can start living life courageously.

A strong woman should never allow anyone to believe they are what is needed for you to feel secure. Security comes from self-confidence, as well as acceptance. Once you accept all your flaws you can begin embracing who you really are. That is the step that will be needed for the opportunity to work on those imperfections.

A strong woman must always believe you are valuable, you are beautiful, and you are courageous. Understand there is nothing you cannot make it through. You are the only one responsible for your self-fulfillment. Obstacles will often arise, and you should never be afraid to face them. Build up that courage and know you have what it takes to conquer through it all.

A strong woman should willingly give another woman a compliment. There should never be hesitation on your part when allowing yourself to acknowledge good qualities of another woman. Having admiration for someone does not take anything away from you, it shows you are full of confidence and that should be your reassurance.

A strong woman must never ever apologize for choosing themselves first. When it is time for decision making, always make sure whatever you decide is beneficial to you. Often too much pride is taken when putting others first, while being comfortable putting yourself last. Try thinking of you more than usual and enjoy it while doing so.

A strong woman should consume all thoughts with positivity while indulging your brain cells with knowledge. Encouraging growth with learning while continuing to expand your mind with the determination needed to stay flourished and focused.

A strong woman knows sometimes the love you give may not always be reciprocated. Believe in yourself by understanding your worth. Realize what you have may be way too much. Do not be so hard on yourself and stop giving love. Just start rechanneling your feelings in a different direction. Understand this is not the end, this is just the beginning of a new lesson and eventually your love will be rewarded by appreciation and returned with interest.

A strong woman often has insecurities when dealing with self-image. If you are not completely happy with your overall look or body image, your self-esteem can begin to deteriorate which can lead to depression.

Although you may be dissatisfied now, there is always an opportunity to change those feelings. Begin by taking time out for yourself, start exercising, or join the new gym. Look into other forms of meditation like yoga or Pilates. It is never too late for you to begin living healthy. It is all about doing what is needed for you to improve your self-esteem. No matter when you decide to make the changes, remember you are beautiful and very courageous to attempt the next step. Keep in mind, giving up should never be an option. Now, stop being so hard on yourself and began working on the strong woman you know you are.

NEW BEGINNINGS

A strong woman understands that anything in life is achievable. Stay determined to get what you need and continue working hard for all that you want. Keep focusing on your goals. Now sit back and watch how your life will begin to shift.

A strong woman knows that life is meant to be lived, for you to reach various levels throughout your journey. To reach your highest peak, you must really want it, be willing to claim it, and have the courage to chase it. Continue moving forward without any hesitation, so your wildest dreams can be captured.

A strong woman should never allow rejection to hinder the dreams that were once inspired. Sometimes a dismissal is needed in order to change a temporary situation. Occasionally, you might have to address the issues at hand, then go on an intense soul search. You may realize that being dismissed was a sign for you to be able to switch positions while obtaining a fresh new start.

A strong woman may often find their calling in life during the oddest times. It can be presented in many ways. Once it appears you must be willing to accept it. You must then step out on faith with a confidant sense of self. Journal on what that calling is while preparing yourself to make your dreams come true.

A strong woman knows most roads ahead will be strewn with obstacles but that may be the only road to your destination. Understand, even if the road takes a sudden detour, be ok with the change. With this new diversion, you may find the most scenic road you ever saw in your life and still arrive at your point of embarkation sooner than you could have ever imagined.

A strong woman must understand getting older just means you are getting wiser. Hopefully, you will begin making better choices, and you will start living life a little more realistic. Age can only help you to mature. It allows you the ability to adapt to new situations while being better at improving them. As you continue to gracefully age, your time here will assist you as you grow while you are rejoicing in the woman you are becoming.

A strong woman must be unapologetic with how you choose to live your life. You only receive one so make it count. Embrace every second, never allowing life's journey to stagnate your growth. Continue learning while living through the ups and downs. Understand things may seem to never get easier but you must keep reinventing yourself to overcome any obstacle you are faced with. Always look for self-improvement and growth because anything that is not being watered will slowly begin dying.

A strong woman needs to remember every day that ends will bring a better and brighter tomorrow. So, begin by loving yourself first, enjoying what you do, while always doing the best that you can. Do it all without any hesitation or regrets.

A strong woman must understand being open to different ideas can expose you to new experiences. It is normal to become comfortable with consistency. Sometimes, you must be willing to step outside of your comfort zone and explore. Exposure is the key to changing and can only add value to your life. Development requires transformation, which will help you to recreate the woman you need to become.

A strong woman must be comfortable enough to love the skin that they are in. There are always going to be a time to criticize things you are not happy about. The same way you can embrace the great qualities you possess. You are always going to have flaws; you must be confident enough to acknowledge them. Stop sitting around complaining about the things you can change. Act now and begin working on the changes that need to be made. Stop allowing that feeling of playing the victim to become so natural, that is no longer acceptable. Fight hard for what you want, so when the story ends you can be remembered not only as a warrior, but also as a BEAUTIFUL SURVIVOR.

Made in the USA
Middletown, DE
06 November 2021